WHOSE VOICE IS TELLING YOU THAT YOUR BODY IS ALL USED UP?

God Still has a plan for the elderly.

By Robert Johnson

Copyright ©2025 Robert Johnson

All rights reserved. No part of this publication may be reproduced, distributed, or transmitted in any form or by any means, including photocopying, recording, or other electronic or mechanical methods, without the prior written permission of the publisher, except in the case of brief quotations embodied in critical reviews and other non-commercial uses permitted by copyright law. For permission requests, write to the publisher at the address below. In accordance with the U.S. Copyright Act of 1976, the scanning, uploading, and electronic sharing of any part of this book without the permission of the publisher is unlawful piracy and theft of the author's intellectual property. Thank you for your support of the author's rights.

Permission: For information on getting permission for reprints

and excerpts, contact:

Hodge Publishing

2001 Timberloch Place, Suite 500

The Woodlands, TX 77380

info@hodgepublishing.com

ISBN: 979-8-3493-4373-5

979-8-9875538-2-4

All scriptures are from the New King James Version of the Bible

unless otherwise indicated.

Scriptures taken from the Holy Bible, New International Version®,

NIV®. Copyright © 1973, 1978, 1984, 2011 by Biblica, Inc.™ Used by

permission of Zondervan. All rights reserved worldwide.

www.zondervan.com The "NIV" and "New Inter-national Version" are trademarks registered in the United States Patent and Trademark Office by Biblica, Inc.®

This book is dedicated to my good and loyal friend, Portia Hebert, who has helped me with writing and preparing this book for publishing.

TABLE OF CONTENTS

Chapter One: Determine Whose Voice Is Talking To You.. 2

Chapter Two: Young Or Old…Does It Matter?........... 5

Chapter Three: How Do You Recover More Quickly? 7

Chapter Four: Let Us Get To Know God, Our Healer 9

Chapter Five: Why Did God Create Us With Limitations?... 11

Chapter Six: Has Anything Spiritual Happened In Your Life? 13

Chapter Seven: Is Jesus Coming For You? 15

Chapter Eight: Are You Aware That You Live In Two Worlds…The Physical One And The Spiritual One?. 17

Chapter Nine: Have You Looked At What's Going On In The World Today? 19

Chapter Ten: Is This God's Plan For The End Of The World…The Doomsday Clock? 21

Chapter Eleven: The Antichrist 25

Chapter Twelve: Worship Of The Beast 37

Chapter Thirteen: How Close Are We To Midnight On The Doomsday Clock And To The End? 40

WHOSE VOICE IS TELLING YOU THAT YOUR BODY IS ALL USED UP?

CHAPTER ONE

DETERMINE WHOSE VOICE IS TALKING TO YOU

Let us start this first chapter with an experience I had a few days ago. I was driving down the highway on my way to the grocery store to pick up a case of water. Once I arrived, I noticed how crowded it was, but I needed that water, so I went ahead and went inside. I managed to get to the back of the store where all the brands of water are kept. I decided to go ahead and get the largest size that contained thirty-two bottles, each having sixteen ounces, all neatly wrapped up in plastic. As I was struggling to pick it up, I noticed how very heavy it was. Once I got it into the basket, I became so short of breath, I was gasping for air.

I have bought this many times before and it was not this hard. What was going on? Why was this so hard on me now? It was like someone had added a hundred pounds to the water.

Once I got my breath and composure back, I managed to get to the register to check out. I slowly rolled the basket down the car aisle to my truck. Again, I struggled to get the water out of the basket into the truck. It took some time and quite a bit of my breath, but I finally managed to get it done.

As I was driving home and thinking about what all had transpired, I heard this voice in my head saying, "STOP doing this! Your body is all used up!" I looked around and no one was there. I was still alone in my truck. Who was that talking to me? The warning and loudness in the voice took me completely off guard.

When I arrived home, I once again struggled to get the water from my truck to my home. While I was putting it down on the floor, once again, I heard that voice, "STOP doing this! Your body is all used up!" Again, I looked around, but no one was there.

At this point, I went to my bedroom and decided to take a quick inventory of myself. Was I losing my mind? Why was I hearing that voice? Who was that talking to me?

I analyzed myself and wrote down some very real facts: I am eighty-two years old. Water weighs over eight pounds per gallon (8.34 to be exact). Thirty-two bottles' times sixteen ounces of water divided by one hundred twenty-eight ounces in a

gallon equals four gallons. Four gallons of water times 8.34 equals 33.36 pounds, plus plastic bottles, plus plastic wrap. I would estimate around thirty-five pounds.

I looked back over the past few months and thought about the times I purchased water. The struggle to lift it has become harder and harder on me. I just did not want to admit it. Surely there must be many others my age and younger who are subject to these hardships and handicaps. I cannot be the only one…can I?

As I began to think more and more about this situation, I felt my heart tugging at me to help others who may also be struggling. So, this is the purpose of this book, to help you through these challenges and difficulties and to learn how to get help.

CHAPTER TWO

YOUNG OR OLD…DOES IT MATTER?

When we are young, we can get sick or injured, and usually we heal much much quicker than we do when we are older. I do not really know why it is like that. Perhaps not for everyone, just for most of us.

If you are younger, your strength will be renewed if you take care of yourself and your health by eating healthy foods, properly exercising, refraining from smoking, alcohol, and narcotics.

Give God praise and thank Him each day for your health and for your youth. Thank Him for guiding and helping you to make the right choices for your health and lifestyle.

As we begin to get older, some of us begin to lose our strength and stamina. We do not realize it at first. It just creeps up on us little by little over the years until one day we realize that our vitality, energy, strength, etc. are gone and they are not coming back.

The best way to take care of our older bodies is to stop overexerting ourselves and ask for help. If we choose to not take care of ourselves, well, we open ourselves up to heart, lung, or other organ issues that may or may not be fatal. We need to take care of our bodies by eating healthy foods, walking, or exercising, refraining from tobacco/smoking, alcohol, and narcotics.

The most powerful method I know of is to pray to God each and every day. It is the absolute best thing you can do. However, remember, God expects us to do our part also. We work with God as a team to optimize our health.

CHAPTER THREE

HOW DO YOU RECOVER MORE QUICKLY?

Let us talk about how to recover more quickly from sickness or injuries. Most people wait until they become sick or injured, then they begin to pray and ask God to heal them. Actually, this may be the only time they ever pray is when they need for God to do something for them.

Some individuals rely only on doctors and pills for healing.

If you want to recover more quickly, wouldn't it be better to have two sources for healing? What about having God and the doctor(s)? When it comes to your health, can you have too many proven sources?

God will always hear your prayers. Why not take inventory of yourself, your heart, and see where you stand with God? What have you got to lose except for your health?

I would like to recommend that you get a good physical check-up with your doctor. Then, go online and research different healthy, natural fruit and vegetable juices, natural healthy supplements such as ginger root, a good liquid vitamin and mineral supplement, a good probiotic that includes a good prebiotic, and then ask your doctor if it is okay for you to take these once you make your choices.

If you eat healthily, you may only need a few. You and your doctor can make the best decisions for you.

Again, most importantly, pray and ask God to direct you, guide you, and help you and your doctor to make the right decisions as to what is the best for you.

CHAPTER FOUR

LET US GET TO KNOW GOD, OUR HEALER

You know, I have read the Bible, and, in the Gospels, Matthew, Mark, Luke, and John, I see where Jesus healed the blind, healed the lame, and healed all kinds of sicknesses. In fact, He even raised people from the dead. Two of these were a twelve-year-old little girl and a man named Lazarus. It took no effort at all on Jesus's part.

Do you know that Jesus still heals today? God is the same today, yesterday, and forever. He never changes…we change…He does not.

The Bible says **in Isaiah 53:5**: "But He was wounded for our transgressions, He was bruised for our iniquities; The chastisement for our peace was upon Him, And by His stripes we are healed. "By the stripes of Jesus, we are healed."

You may be saying to yourself, "why does God heal some and not others?" The Bible says in **Isaiah 55:8-9**: "For my thoughts are not your thoughts, neither are your ways my ways, saith the LORD. For as the heavens are higher than the earth, so are my ways higher than your ways, and my thoughts than your thoughts".

In this passage, God's "ways" refer to his divine plans and purposes, which are superior to human ways. This phrase is a reminder to trust in God's plan, especially when we do not understand what or why something is happening.

We do not know the answers to everything. I do not believe we are supposed to know. We are to trust God and believe in Him and His Word, giving Him praise and thanks each and every day.

God knows what our future holds…we do not. When we serve and trust God, He takes care of our future and of us.

CHAPTER FIVE

WHY DID GOD CREATE US WITH LIMITATIONS?

Why do we have limitations? When our Father God created us, He did not create us just to leave us out here on our own. We are created to need God, His fellowship, His blessings, and His healing in our lives on a daily basis.

This life is brutal with all its pressures, hurts, pestilences, diseases, worries, wars, and rumors of wars that fight against our bodies and from birth to old age. Some individuals are so overwrought with doctor appointments, pills, surgeries, mental handicaps, family deaths, loneliness, just to name a few, that they can hardly cope as they get older.

We are limited in many aspects of our lives. God has no limits! **Luke 1:37** says, "For nothing will be impossible with God." This verse is a summary of the hope that comes from faith in God. Try turning it around…without God, nothing will be possible.

God is our all in all. God is the completion of our limitations.

CHAPTER SIX

HAS ANYTHING SPIRITUAL HAPPENED IN YOUR LIFE?

We all know that God, our Healer, is also the God of miracles and spiritual experiences.

Do you want to see a miracle? Look around at the sky, the birds, life, and look at your own body. Only a Divine Creator could create a body so intricately made as a human's. If God did not form us, as the Bible says He did, why isn't your nose where your foot is? Why isn't your head where your leg is? Why do your lungs automatically breathe keeping you alive? I will tell you why... In **Jeremiah 1:5** God says, "Before I formed you in the womb, I knew you; before you were born, I sanctified you; and I ordained you a prophet to the nations." Sadly, this is one of those verses that a lot of people hate because it clearly brings to our attention the sovereignty and control of God.

Let us talk about supernatural healing from God through faith in Jesus Christ. With these two sources, you are well on your way to healing.

Prayer, faith, and trust is what you need to condition your mind and heart which results in a prosperous prayer. Jesus Christ suffered and died on the cross for all of us, so this is a win, win situation for all of us. We only need to ask him to forgive us for our sins, to come into our hearts, and we must turn away from sinning.

Did you know that you can also ask Him for healing, guidance, deliverance, direction, and help to know and follow His will? Did you know you can ask Him to help you in your daily life, your job, with your relatives, friends, and any situation that comes up? He is always right by your side to help you. Psalms 16:8 says: "I know the Lord is always with me. I will not be shaken, for He is right beside me." All through the New Testament, Jesus says that He will always be with us.

When God answers our prayers, whether the way we want Him to or not, we need to thank Him and praise Him. If we trust in His love for us, we can do this.

CHAPTER SEVEN

IS JESUS COMING FOR YOU?

Have you ever thought about where you will go when you die?

God truly wants to connect with you. However, he has left it entirely in your hands. He is allowing you to make the choice of whether to have Him in your life or not. He also gives you the choice of whether you want to spend eternity with Him in heaven or eternity in hell without Him. God does not send anyone to hell. We send ourselves by rejecting His son, Jesus Christ. **John 3:16** says, "For God so loved the world that He gave His only begotten Son, that whoever believes in Him should not perish but have everlasting life".

Some people simply do not know how to connect with God. Others do not want to try. It is simple. Just talk with God like you are talking to a Father who loves and adores you, because He does.

Prayer time with God, reading your Bible, and Christian fellowship are all great ways to help you build your faith and relationship with Jesus Christ.

CHAPTER EIGHT

ARE YOU AWARE THAT YOU LIVE IN TWO WORLDS...THE PHYSICAL ONE AND THE SPIRITUAL ONE?

The big picture in this book is about you. Many of you know there are two worlds...the physical world and the spiritual world. Did you know that the physical world is controlled by the spiritual world? Are you aware that good and evil spirits are always at work in our lives every day?

You can choose to fill your mind and heart with positive, life flowing good by reading the Bible, praying, choosing Christian fellowship, focusing on things in our lives that will please God. This helps us to avoid evil forces coming into our lives and trying to influence us to disobey God and to commit sin. Ask God to forgive you of your sins and to help you be reborn of the Holy Spirit. As Jesus to save you from going to hell.

Or you can choose to fill your mind and heart with negativity, sin, evil and everything that goes against God and His son Jesus Christ. It is your choice. God only wants someone who chooses to love Him like He loves us. You can reject Him and His son, Jesus Christ, who died for the awful sins you committed, and well, you will be choosing hell over heaven when you die and pass from this earth. It is up to you.

I would strongly suggest that you read the two books, "The End Has Already Passed, Why Are You Still Here?" and "How to Talk to God and How to Find Favor with God," by Robert D. Johnson. I also suggest you read, "A Divine Revelation of Hell" by Mary K. Baxter. All three of these books are a must read.

What have you got to lose? Once you have read them, then make your decision.

CHAPTER NINE

HAVE YOU LOOKED AT WHAT'S GOING ON IN THE WORLD TODAY?

Look around! What do you see on the news? What do you see or hear about on television and radio? What are your friends and neighbors talking about?

As we look at the news media, we see a world that is falling apart. The bad news of the world is going on seven days a week, twenty-four hours a day. Wars are happening in most of the world, some for many years, and others threatening to start a war. There appears to be no end in sight. The world appears to be at its end, and we are right in the middle of it.

The Bible talks about all of this. All of this was prophesied thousands of years ago in Matthew 24:6-13:" You will hear of wars and rumors of wars but see to it that you are not alarmed. Such things must happen, but the end is still to come. Nation will rise against nation, and kingdom against kingdom. There will be famines and earthquakes in various places. All these are the beginning of birth pains. Then you will be handed over to be persecuted and put to death, and you will be hated by all nations because of me. At that time many will turn away from the faith and will betray and hate each other, and many false prophets will appear and deceive many people. Because of the increase of wickedness, the love of most will grow cold, but the one who stands firm to the end will be saved."

The Books of Isaiah, Ezekiel, Revelation, and all throughout the Bible tell of the things that must come and that are happening right now...at this very time. Are you ready for it? Have you made your choice?

It is definitely time for all of us to do something for ourselves, as is strongly pointed out in this book. Read this book and the other books I recommended. Read your Bible. Pray and talk to your Heavenly Father each and every day. Remember, He gave His one and only Son for you, for all of us, out of His love.

CHAPTER TEN

IS THIS GOD'S PLAN FOR THE END OF THE WORLD...THE DOOMSDAY CLOCK?

Do you know what the Doomsday Clock is?

In 1947, artist and Bulletin member Martyl Langsdorf created the iconic Doomsday Clock to signal how close humanity was to self-destruction. Today, the Doomsday Clock is located at the Bulletin offices in the Keller Center, home to the University of Chicago Harris School of Public Policy.

- **What it is**

    The Doomsday Clock is a clock face with hands that indicate how close the world is to a global catastrophe. The Bulletin of the Atomic Scientists adjusts the minute hand of the clock each year.

- **Why it was created**

    The Bulletin of the Atomic Scientists created the Doomsday Clock in 1947 as a way to gauge how close humanity was to a civilizational collapse. The Bulletin's mission is to inform the public about man-made threats.

- **What it means**

    The Bulletin says the Doomsday Clock is a reminder of the perils that humanity must address to survive on the planet. The clock's time conveys how close humanity is to destroying civilization with dangerous technologies.

- **2024 time**

In 2024, the Bulletin kept the clock set at 90 seconds to midnight.

The Doomsday Clock is set every year by the Bulletin's Science and Security Board in consultation with its Board of Sponsors, which includes nine Nobel laureates. The Clock has become a universally recognized indicator of the world's vulnerability to global catastrophe caused by man-made technologies.

Why is the Doomsday Clock at 90 seconds to midnight? In 2023, the clock moved its closest to midnight – just 90 seconds away. The organization said the update was made "largely (though not exclusively) because of the mounting dangers of the war in Ukraine.

The Doomsday Clock pictured at its setting of "90 seconds to midnight", last changed in January 2024

Frequency   Annually

Inaugurated   June 1947

Most recent   **January 23, 2024**

Why is the Doomsday Clock pointless? Potentially, most importantly, the Doomsday Clock has, more than anything, failed to recognize changes in how nuclear weapons are perceived and treated by national governments. Nuclear weapons were seen as a significant threat in the late 1940's because they had recently been used in Japan.

Whether valid or not, the Doomsday Clock is not about your own clock ticking away the hours, minutes, and seconds even though they are somewhat connected.

CHAPTER ELEVEN

THE ANTICHRIST

Before the ninety seconds on the Doomsday Clock expires, The Antichrist will appear. He will be voted as head of the United Nations because of his ability to bring peace to the Middle East. He will promise Israel peace. He will rule this world for seven years.

Christians need to be aware of antichrists within our midst. How do we recognize those who are antichrists? By looking through the lens of God's Word! **1 John 2:22** says, "Who is a liar but he who denies that Jesus is the Christ? He is antichrist who denies the Father and the Son." Those who claim there is no God and/or that Jesus is not the Son of God but just another man, and teach men so, are antichrists. "And every spirit that does not confess that Jesus Christ has come in the flesh is not of God. And this is the spirit of Antichrist, which you have heard was coming, and is now already in the world" **1 John 4:3**. Those who would claim the Messiah is not Jesus or that Jesus never really came are also considered to be antichrists. They clearly teach doctrine contrary to the Bible. **2 John 1:7** tells us, "For many deceivers have gone out into the world who do not confess Jesus Christ as coming in the flesh. This is a deceiver and an antichrist."

Two other terms used in Scripture to describe the two types of antichrists are "man of sin" and "the son of perdition." "Man of sin" describes the Antichrist, and the term "son of perdition" is used for both the Antichrist and antichrists, as seen in these two passages. **2 Thessalonians 2:3-4** says, "Let no one deceive you by any means; for that Day will not come unless the falling away comes first, and *the man of sin* is revealed, *the son of perdition*, who opposes and exalts himself above all that is called God or that is worshipped, so that he sits as God in the temple of God, showing himself that he is God." In this verse, we see that the Antichrist is called by both terms and how he desires to be worshipped as God. In this next verse, we see Jesus refer to Judas Iscariot by the term son of perdition. This is further proof that Judas was never one of Jesus' own, but a deceiver, an antichrist. "While I was with them in the world, I kept them in Your name. Those whom You gave me I have kept; and none of them is lost except the son of perdition, that the Scripture might be fulfilled" (**John 17:12**).

There are a lot of people who are on the fence about whether to accept the Lord Jesus Christ as their personal God and Savior. There are others who oppose and deny Jesus as the Christ. We need to focus on "Where is He?" Where is Jesus, what is He doing and how can I serve Him?" Those are the questions we need to focus on. Read His Word and learn of Him who saves. Study the Word of God (your Bible), study the Truth in your Bible, and you will be able to recognize a lie when it is before you. The Holy Spirit will help you.

I have a hard time understanding why or how anyone could reject or deny Jesus. It was easy for me to choose a loving Savior who took all my sins upon Himself and went through unimaginable torment, beatings, humiliation, pain, and suffering and then to die on a cross to keep me from going to hell. He took the punishment that I deserved, that all of us deserved. For all of us have lied, thought sinful thoughts, and sinned in some way against God. It says in **Romans 3:23**: ²³ "for all have sinned and fall short of the glory of God,"

I could never have paid that debt! It was easy for me to see the only way to spend eternity with God, my Father, was to accept His precious Son, Jesus, as my Lord and Savior. **John 3:16-18**: "This is how much God loved the world: He gave His Son, His one and only Son. And this is why; so that no one need be destroyed; by believing in Him, anyone can have a whole and lasting life. God did not go to all the trouble of sending His Son merely to point an accusing finger, telling the world how bad it was. He came to help, to put the world right again. Anyone who trusts in Him is acquitted; anyone who refuses to trust Him has long since been under the death sentence without knowing it. And why? Because of that person's failure to believe in the one and only Son of God when introduced to Him."

When God resurrected Jesus from the dead, the power and importance of the Jesus's voluntary death for us is inexhaustible. He voluntarily gave

His life for you, for me, and for all of us. He surrendered His Spirit to God, then the curtain split. There was

a terrible earthquake that split rocks and opened tombs. Many people saw the bodies of saints who were raised by Jesus enter the city. The results of Jesus voluntarily and willingly giving His life and death are as real today as ever. History will come to a final close. Then, we will be singing the song of the Lamb of God that was slain. **Revelation 5:9-13:** 9 "And they sang a new song, saying, "Worthy are you to take the scroll and to open its seals, for you were slain, and by your blood you ransomed people for God from every tribe and language and people and nation and

you have made them a kingdom and priests to our God, and they shall reign on the

earth." Then, I looked, and I heard around the throne and the living creatures and the elders the voice of many angels, numbering myriads of myriads and thousands of thousands, saying with a loud voice, "Worthy is the Lamb who was slain, to receive power and wealth and wisdom and might and honor and glory and blessing!"

And I heard every creature in heaven and on earth and under the earth and in the sea, and all that is in them, saying, "To him who sits on the throne and to the Lamb be blessing and honor and glory and might forever and ever!"

God is bringing this world to an end. We are watching everything play out in our world today just as the Bible foretold long long ago. We are living deep in the Book of Revelation and, sadly, the world situation is not going to get any better. It is only going to get much worse!

The evil forces in our world are controlling evil beings and those who have rejected Christ. They are bringing about chaos, destruction, killings, and warring against those who have chosen Jesus Christ as their Savior. Many have fallen away from their faith in Jesus Christ.

God is going to bring all of this to an end very soon. I believe, He is going to take those of us who choose Jesus as Lord and Savior out of this world before the Great Tribulation begins. I believe at the 11/100th of a second on the Doom's Day Clock, believers from all over the world will be taken up into the air to meet Jesus. The Rapture - the raising of the Church into heaven (**1 Thessalonians 4:17**)—is the next event on the prophetic calendar. The Rapture is when Christ comes back and takes every Christian that is still on this earth and resurrects all of those who have died and takes them to heaven with Him. In **1 Thessalonians 5:1-8**, Paul expresses that the Lord's return will be like a thief in the night. No one knows the date or time. However, there are several signs of the End Times that we can all be aware of. Events such as earthquakes and diseases, wars and dispute among nations, and persecution against Israel and Christians are all signs leading to the Rapture.

Matthew 24:40-42: "Two men will be in the field; one will be taken and the other left. Two women will be grinding with a hand mill; one will be taken and the other left. "Therefore, keep watch, because you do not know on what day your Lord will come. "

1 Corinthians 15:51–53: "Listen, I tell you a mystery: We will not all sleep, but we will all be changed— in a flash, in the twinkling of an eye, at the last trumpet. For the trumpet will sound, the dead will be raised imperishable, and we will be changed. For the perishable must clothe itself with the imperishable, and the mortal with immortality."

1 Thessalonians 4:13-18: "Brothers and sisters, we do not want you to be uninformed about those who sleep in death, so that you do not grieve like the rest of mankind, who have no hope. For we believe that Jesus died and rose again, and so we believe that God will bring with Jesus those who have fallen asleep in him. According to the Lord's word, we tell you that we who are still alive, who are left until the coming of the Lord, will certainly not precede those who have fallen asleep. For the Lord himself will come down from heaven, with a loud command, with the voice of the archangel and with the trumpet call of God, and the dead in Christ will rise first. After that, we who are still alive and are left will be caught up together with them in the clouds to meet the Lord in the air. And so, we will be with the Lord forever. Therefore encourage one another with these words."

Watch for soon coming military changes as things get even worse in our world. The Antichrist will rule this world for seven years. The United Nations will elect him to rule the world because of his seemingly successful peace efforts. The Antichrist will appear as a man and claim to be God. He will be powerful, and he will control the entire world. **Daniel 7:25**: "He will speak great words against the most High and wear out the saints of the most High and think to change times and laws."

"And I saw a beast rising out of the sea, with ten horns and seven heads, with ten diadems on its horns and blasphemous names on its heads. And the beast that I saw was like a leopard; its feet were like a bear's, and its mouth was like a lion's mouth. And to it the dragon gave his power and his throne and great authority."

"Then I saw another beast rising out of the earth. It had two horns like a lamb, and it spoke like a dragon. It exercises all the authority of the first beast in its presence and makes the earth and its inhabitants worship the first beast, whose mortal wound was healed. It performs great signs, even making fire come down from heaven to earth in front of people, and by the signs that it is allowed to work in the presence of the beast it deceives those who dwell on earth, telling them to make an image for the beast that was wounded by the sword and yet lived. And it was allowed to give breath to the image of the beast, so that the image of the beast might even speak and might cause those who would not worship the image of the beast to be slain. Also, it causes all, both small and great, both rich and poor, both free and slave, to be marked on the right hand or the forehead, so that no one can buy or sell unless he has the mark, that is, the name of the beast or the number of its name. This calls for wisdom: let the one who has understanding calculate the number of the beast, for it is the number of a man, and his number is 666.—

Revelation 13:1, 2; 11–18

At the end of the first three and one-half years, the Antichrist will be wounded and die. Satan will bring him back to life and take over his body, mind, thoughts, and his very soul totally and completely. He will look and appear like a man, but he will be Satan. Everyone will worship him and believe that he is God. He will perform many miracles. He will deceive many.

Then, he will require everyone to take his mark on either their forehead or their right hand. Only those who take his mark will be allowed to buy, sell, work. If anyone refuses his mark, they will be executed…probably beheaded for others to see in order to scare them into taking his demonic mark. Loyalty and, ultimately worship of the beast, as evidenced by the taking of his "mark," is considered blasphemy toward God. **Revelation 14** spells out the impact for those who choose to take the mark of the beast. **Revelation 14:9b-11** "If anyone worships the beast and its image and receives a mark on his forehead or on his hand… he will be tormented with fire and sulfur in the presence of the holy angels and in the presence of the Lamb. And the smoke of their torment goes up forever and ever, and they have no rest, day or night, these worshipers of the beast and its image, and whoever receives the mark of its name."

It is important to study the Bible intently as we try to discern God's perfect will for our lives, both today and as we approach an uncertain future.

Please DO NOT TAKE THE MARK!!!

CHAPTER TWELVE

WORSHIP OF THE BEAST

The staying power of the beast and its empire leads to worship of the dragon and the beast. The dragon is worshiped for giving authority to the beast. The beast is worshiped because of his so-called resurrection. He is considered incomparable and omnipotent, like God. People worship the beast, believing he cannot be resisted or overcome. As has often been observed in history, people stand with a winner.

Twice in this verse we are told what "was given" to the beast: a mouth to utter proud, blasphemous words, and authority for forty-two months. Although the dragon actively gives his authority over to the beast (the Antichrist), God reigns and rules over what the beast carries out, allowing or permitting the beast to exercise his authority. Even though God ordains what the beast does, he does not have the same motivations or intent as Satan. God's judgment is his mysterious way of handling and controlling things. **(Isa. 28:21)** God always calls on and desires for the wicked to repent and live **(Ezek. 18:23, 32).** Satan always rejoices when people are destroyed.

The beast is full of evil, uttering "haughty and blasphemous words" against God. Such activity fits also with the "man of lawlessness," who exalts himself as divine **(2 Thess. 2:3–4).** The beast will be allowed to exercise his authority for forty-two months. Some understand this to be a literal three and one-half years before Jesus returns. But John is more likely describing the entire period between Jesus' first and second coming.

The beast opposes God and his people. The beast will harbor hate towards anything and anyone devoted to the one true and living God.

God does reign and rule over the Beast. God has allowed him to make war on the saints and conquer them. This does not mean the saints surrender their faith, although, sadly, some will. It means God allows the beast to take their lives. "This horn made war with the saints and prevailed over them" **(Dan. 7:21-25)**. God grants the desires of the beast for a period of time, so that the beast exercises authority over every tribe, tongue, people, and nation.

However, if you read the end of the Book of Revelation, you will see that God and His Son, Jesus Christ rule and reign for eternity. All of us who refuse the mark of the Beast and refuse to worship him will be overcomers and spend eternity with God, our Father. Jesus Christ is now and always will be the King of Kings and the Lord of Lords.

Won't you ask Him into your heart now? Ask Him to forgive your sins and commit your life to Him. He stands at the door of your heart, knocking. I pray you open the door and invite Him in before it is too late.

CHAPTER THIRTEEN

HOW CLOSE ARE WE TO MIDNIGHT ON THE DOOMSDAY CLOCK AND TO THE END?

Let us take a look at the world and see how close we are to all of this happening in our lifetime.

According to the news media of a few days ago, all of our military weapons are totally depleted since we give so much away to help other countries whose people are being killed in wars. An example of this is Ukraine. We do need to help these countries and all of their suffering people to fight against evil.

If we were attacked by other countries like Russia, China, and/or North Korea, how would we stand up? If nuclear weapons of mass destruction are used, it would be game over for all of us on earth. This would be the beginning of World War III. This is when the Antichrist comes on the scene to prevent the world from destroying itself, and he will then begin to take over the world.

In addition to all of this, Russia has apparently made it very clear that if they lose this war with Ukraine, they are going to start a nuclear war. At this point in time, this country, Germany, Poland, and all the other countries will be sending tanks, missiles, drones, and other heavy-duty war winning military equipment to Ukraine.

Remember, the Bible is based around Israel. According to the Bible, the entire world will turn against Israel in the last days. Isn't that what is happening now? Hamas and its evil attacked and savagely murdered innocent babies by cutting their heads off. They brutally beat and raped women and then murdered them. The had no feeling when they killed innocent men, women, and children all because of their hatred for Israel. The UN, college students, and many individuals seem to be blinded to the evil horrid behavior of Hamas. How can they turn against Israel for what Hamas has done? This is truly a sign of the end times.

Zechariah 12:3 On that day I will make Jerusalem a heavy stone for all the peoples. All who lift it will surely hurt themselves. And all the nations of the earth will gather against it.

Zechariah 14:1-21 Behold, a day is coming for the LORD, when the spoil taken from you will be divided in your midst. For I will gather all the Jerusalem to battle, and the city shall be taken and the houses plundered, and the women raped. Half of the city shall go out into exile, but the rest of the people shall not be cut off from the city. Then the LORD will go out and fight against those nations as when he fights on a day of battle. On that day his feet shall stand on the Mount of Olives that lies before Jerusalem on the east, and the Mount of Olives shall be split in two from east to west by a very wide valley, so that one half of the Mount shall move northward, and the other half southward. And you shall flee to the valley of my mountains, for the valley of the mountains shall reach Azal. And you shall flee as you fled from the earthquake in the days of Uzziah king of Judah. Then the LORD my God will come, and all the holy ones with him. .....

The Battle of Armageddon will be the final showdown between good and evil on earth. After the Tribulation, Jesus will return to earth as a mighty King with the armies of heaven to destroy all those who have rejected Him as Savior. The forces of evil will rally the nations against Him. There will be no bystanders—the entire earth will be involved.

Jesus will defeat the Antichrist and his False Prophet quickly, but the Bible describes the battle in detail.

There is only one way out of the coming tribulation and the evil with it. It is a decision that you and you alone must make. You can choose to be a part of the evil that is soon coming, or you can choose Jesus Christ as your personal Lord and Savior.

If you choose Jesus as your personal Lord and Savior, simply pray in your own words now. Millions of us have gladly done this before you. Tell Jesus that you know you are a sinner and that you have sinned against Him and His Holy Laws. Ask Jesus to forgive you and come into your heart and life and save you. Let Him know that you come humbly before him with an open heart in all humility. Let Him know that as you look at the world situation and how it is today, you realize that you need him now and forever. Amen.

This is the real deal! Please do not send yourself to hell by rejecting Jesus as your Savior. He is so willing to forgive you for your sins. After all, He voluntarily gave His life for you. He suffered for you. He rose from the dead so that you could be raised from the dead to be with Him forever. He stands waiting…knocking at the door of your heart.

Let's meet up in heaven. I will be looking for you.

Robert

www.ingramcontent.com/pod-product-compliance
Lightning Source LLC
LaVergne TN
LVHW051924060526
838201LV00062B/4677